Improving
Mem

How to Drastically Improve Memory

Blueleo Media

By Cameron Ferguson

TABLE OF CONTENTS

INTRODUCTION

When people experience serious memory problems, they are recommended to ask for medical advice from a certified doctor. The medic will teach people how to improve memory. Some severe diseases, such as Alzheimer's disease or dementia are preceded by episodes of memory loss.

This is why the persons who experience memory loss are advised to speak to a doctor. However, people can find many other valuable resources that show them how to preserve the memory.

By learning about how to improve memory, people can treat a memory loss problem, but most importantly, they can prevent such undesirable conditions.

You want to learn how to improve memory because we've all had problems with it. Memory loss, memory failure, impairment... whatever you call it, none of it is fun. However, there's one thing that usually causes memory issues that are benign and not as a result of disease.

We all go through phases when we can't recall that specific fact we want to, or are less facile with memory than we used to be. When you feel like memory problems are beginning to happen for you, it's time to take stock and follow some tips that will help you retain your memory. This article will focus on how to improve memory by providing some tips and useful information.

A lot of the time, if we are not interested in something or if it's not funny or particularly bizarre so that it's memorable, it's not going to appeal to us. If something doesn't appeal to your interest, you're not going to retain it.

Therefore, if you don't pay attention to something presented to you, you're not going to remember it. How do you retain a good memory in the first place? You need to keep your full attention on something and keep practicing good memory habits. A lot of the time, though, we fail to do just this.

Listen, if you can learn more and remember things better by using audio media, use this to retain information. This can help you keep yourself apprised of the things around you and it's not too hard to dovetail this with your best learning style; hearing is generally a natural asset to you in the first place.

With so much to remember, keep some focus and work on keeping it all together. This is most important for things like meetings, events, dates and other specific information.

You can name these with phrases or catchy words that will help you remember so that you won't have to look them up or refer to a written list every time. Simply utilizing memorable or catchy phrases can help you associate things with important dates and events.

From time to time, check and see what you need to do on a given day, such as tomorrow. Don't put off doing these small things to try to "protect" your memory, because you can always find a solution to memory problems if you simply focus and concentrate on things.

We all speak of memory as that cerebral process by which we recall or remember something from our previous experience. But did you know that our memories fall into different categories depending on when and how they were formed, and how they are recalled?

Two Primary Types

This part is easy: we have short-term and long-term memories. Short-term is similar to "working memory", in which we remember something long enough to make use of it, then either discard it or commit it to long-term.

A phone number, a short grocery list, and even the beginning of a sentence all fall into this category. You can think of it as the brain's "scratch pad", recording information just long enough to use it.

Long-term memories, are, of course, anything we remember for more than a few minutes. They can be strong (easy to recall) or weak (hard to recall), and are actually not set in stone, but are somewhat fluid.

Our long-term memories are subject to suggestion and to being joined with other memories, so they're not always necessarily accurate. They generally fall into one of two subcategories: explicit (or declarative) and implicit (or nondeclarative), though a given memory may be a mix of both.

Explicit

These are the memories which require conscious thought, such as remembering birthdays, names, and facts, and it's what most people are thinking of when they comment that their memory is good or bad. These memories are usually associated with other things or memories, which helps to maintain the memory and recall it.

Of explicit memories, we have yet another two divisions: episodic and semantic. Episodic memories are your autobiographical, personal memories that only you have.

These types of memories are often stronger when the event happened during a highly emotionally charged situation, like where you were and what you were doing when you heard about the attacks on the World Trade Center on 9/11. These memories often get weaker and less accurate over time as we recall them.

Semantic memories, on the other hand, are about general knowledge of the world, the facts we know without necessarily knowing where or how we learned them, such as knowing what elephants look like and that London is in England. These memories actually get stronger over time.

Implicit Memories

These are a bit more difficult to grasp, since these are the memories we don't consciously think about, we just do. Anything we do "automatically" can fall into this category, and these can get weaker with time. Again, we have two more divisions: procedural and priming.

Procedural memories are about how to perform tasks which we've learned so well we don't really need to consciously think about them any more--like riding a bike or tying a shoelace.

Even everyday actions such as walking re□uire procedural memory. It is possible to loose other parts of your memory, like episodic memory, and still retain procedural memory.

Priming can also bring about implicit memories by relating a memory to your experiences. Whatever you've heard, seen or experienced most recently or most often will be most likely to be connected to an implicit memory, and can thus be an "primer" for that memory.

All brain function is closely connected to health. Exercise, nutrition, and supplementation all play a part in keeping your brain working its best.

Classification of memory loss can be made using many criteria. Depending on the duration, the types of memory loss are permanent and temporary memory loss.

When a certain type of memory is affected, the memory loss can be classified as either short-term memory loss or long-term memory loss. The condition may develop gradually or may appear suddenly. All these types of memory loss are conditioned by certain factors.

Global amnesia is one of the most freȘuent types of memory loss. It is characterized by inability to recall things that are stored in the long-term memory. However, patients who suffer from amnesia do not present any problems related to the short-term memory. Furthermore, amnesiacs can remember semantic memories.

As a proof of this fact, people who suffer from amnesia still know the meanings of the words and information about the general world. This certain type of amnesia is usually provoked by damage inflicted on the medial temporal lobes.

Also, it can appear if the diencephalon or the basal forebrain is affected. The main causes are represented by infections of the brain and by cerebrovascular accidents. Global amnesia is one of the permanent types of memory loss.

A classification of memory loss can also be made after observing the rate of forgetting. This rate depends on the certain part of the brain that is damaged. As many studies have shown, people with medial temporal lobe damage lose memory faster than the diencephalic patients.

Organic amnesia is one of the memory loss types that appear as a result of a brain lesion. It can be found in one or more of the four possible situations. Anterograde amnesia refers to the incapacity to recall events that happen after memory loss is installed.

Retrograde amnesia is the term used when people cannot remember events that have happened before the appearance of memory loss. In the third situation, the intelligence is kept, while in the fourth situation the short-term memory is good. When all these four situations occur simultaneously, people are called global amnesics.

Mild cognitive impairment refers to all the subtle, yet measurable memory conditions. Dementia represents an alteration of the mental processes. Memory is affected in most of the cases of dementia.

Alzheimer's disease is a specific type of dementia which features memory loss always. Vascular dementia is determined by repeated strokes. All these types of memory disorder may provoke a particular type of memory loss.

Many people will have memory lapses from time to time. Most of the time, it's a small detail that is forgotten, or a fact that can't quite make it past the tip of the tongue. True memory loss, however, can be a scary thing, and can be a sign of more serious underlying problems.

Whether the trouble is with short-term or long-term memory, if you notice problems remembering facts, figures or faces, the first step is to contact your physician.

A trained medical professional has the expertise to take a thorough history, perform a physical examination, and order appropriate testing to identify any pathologic cause for your memory issues, as well as provide therapy to restore your health. Some causes of memory problems can be quite serious, so it is crucial to take action right away.

Listed below are several potential causes of memory loss.

Stroke: Stroke, or a cerebrovascular accident (CVA), can have serious impacts on your memory. A stroke occurs when a portion of the brain is deprived of oxygen, or if there is bleeding into a section of the cerebrum.

A person's deficits, as well as their permanence, depend on several factors, including the cause of the stroke, as well as the portion of the brain that is affected. Sometimes people can have difficulty with short-term or long-term memory.

Still other people can have difficulty learning new information, so there is a problem storing memories. Strokes are extremely dangerous and require immediate attention and potentially long-term rehabilitation.

Psychoactive Substance Abuse: Stroke maybe one of the leading causes for short term memory loss among older people but you can see recall problems in younger people as well. Psychoactive substance abuse is considered as a major cause for memory loss among youngsters. Alcohol, drugs and marijuana can cause serious short term memory loss.

While many people are quite aware of the health risks associated with drugs like cocaine and heroin, it's common to underestimate the health impacts of alcohol and marijuana. The latter also can significantly affect a person's memory by sabotaging concentration and causing cell damage.

Inhalant abuse is another abused substance popular with some teens which can also have serious detrimental effects on the brain.

Trauma: Concussions, which are contusions of the brain, can happen with even mild closed head injuries. Some common symptoms of post-concussion syndrome are headaches, nausea, dizziness, difficulty concentrating, and yes, memory-problems. The more severe the trauma, of course, the greater the effect that an injury can have on memory.

Oxygen Deprivation: Intentional or unintentional oxygen deprivation can cause serious damage to the brain. Asphyxiation with bags or choking, or with exposure to harmful chemicals and gases can lead to problems with memory.

Depression: Many people are surprised to learn that depression can present with memory problems. An inability to concentrate is a hallmark of depression, and this can lead to inattention and difficulty taking in the details that will need to be remembered later.

Alzheimer's disease: Alzheimer's disease is a degenerative condition of the brain for which millions of dollars in research are spent every year. Alzheimer's is a form of dementia where people lose much of their memory and forget major portions of their lives. They also have significant difficulty with short-term memory.

Heavy Metal Poisoning: Lead and other heavy metals can cause big problems for brain development and cognitive function with prolonged exposure. This exposure is usually environmental, but can occur with certain occupations or hobbies as well.

These are some of the leading causes for memory loss. Early identification is crucial in all of these conditions, and it is essential to recruit the help of medical professionals to identify and treat the underlying problem.

Your lifestyle can either contribute to your having a healthy well functioning brain, or cause your brain to decline in powers such as memory, cognition and focus. Bad habits like eating a poor diet, drinking too much alcohol, not getting enough sleep, and exposure to too much stress, can greatly affect brain function. This will become worse as you age.

Some lifestyle factors which can affect your brain function and cause it to decline are:

Lack of exercise - If you live a sedentary lifestyle, you risk a decline in brain function along with a decline in your physical health. It all works together. Studies have shown that physical activity is connected to mental sharpness.

Physical activity has a number of positive effects on your brain. It provides a healthy flow of blood through the circulatory system, which includes the brain. It also produces endorphins which stimulate your brain.

Poor diet choices - In addition to keeping your weight at a desirable level, a healthy diet provides nutrients that help your brain by fighting against free radicals that cause inflammation and deterioration of brain functions.

Obesity and bad health from a poor diet may result in long-term diseases such as Alzheimer's disease and other types of dementia. A diet like the Mediterranean is well rounded and keeps the oxygen flowing uninhibited through the brain.

Lack of sleep - Sleep may become a problem, especially as you age. It can be caused by responsibilities which keep you up and going, stress that has you thinking negative thoughts, or physical or mental impairments.

Lack of sleep can greatly affect your brain function by causing lack of focus, memory loss, irritability and fatigue. Your brain performs poorly when these factors keep you from getting enough sleep.

Lack of socialization and feelings of isolation - These two lifestyle factors go hand-in-hand when a person isolates him or herself and doesn't socialize with friends and family. This often happens with age. Retirement occurs and friends and family drift away or pass away. Illness may also be a factor. Both can cause the brain to deteriorate.

Too much stress - Stress comes in many forms. It's part of life, but if it lasts too long and/or is very severe, it can begin to cause both physical and mental problems. Think about ways to alter your lifestyle to get rid of some of the stress in your life.

time for your brain to rest and rejuvenate itself. You'll find that your focus and cognitive powers will be improved. And your brain will have the energy to function as it should.

Other bad habits that might contribute to a decline in brain function include smoking and drinking too much alcohol. Check your lifestyle. See if your brain might be suffering some decline because of bad habits you've developed.

The brain is made up of billions of nerve cells called neurons. These specialized cells are able to process and convey information to other neurons by connecting to form a network. Through these connections neurons are able to receive information from one another.

These networks are responsible for controlling our behaviors and experiences. As the human brain develops, neural networks recognize and reinforce themselves in response to constant stimulation and new learning experiences. This interaction between body and mind is what stimulates neurons to grow and connect with each other in intricate ways.

HOW CONNECTED IS YOUR BRAIN?

A healthy, well-function neuron can be directly linked to tens of thousands of other neurons, creating many more connections. These connections that are made within the brain are the structural foundation for the brains memory capacity and thinking ability.

HOW DO WE STORE MEMORY?

When we experience something our neurons are affected and altered, and a trace or pattern is left in these effected neurons. Repetition of the experience or recall of the event reinforces this link between neurons. Further recall based on the memory makes this link even stronger than before.

This is known as long term potentiation. Long term potentiation refers to a process where connection between two neurons is strengthened, due to the two neurons being continuously active together, this means that over time activity in one neuron will tend to produce activity in the other neuron.

An example of how these connections can be reinforced is the process of remembering a person's name. When you are first introduced to a person their name may be gone from your memory within a few minutes. However if this memory is reinforced by meeting the person on more than one occasion, the memory can persist for much longer.

AGING EFFECTS OF NEURONS

Our neural networks are in a constant state of change. As we age the 100 billion neurons that we are born with gradually die. Disease can further destroy neurons and their connections.

This is why exposing ourselves to new stimuli and challenging our mind is important, as it reinforces and strengthens our existing neural networks. Participating in regular physical activity is also important as it counteracts many of the factors that interfere with healthy neurons.

WORK OUT YOUR MEMORY

Exercise is a key factor in keeping your mind healthy and active thus protecting your memory and preventing the onset of many degenerative memory disorders.

Factors that negatively affect neurons including stress, lack of stimulation and neurotoxins, hinder their ability to form new connections with other neurons and destroy existing connections. These factors can all be counteracted by the positive effects of exercise.

Physical activity is important in maintaining a healthy memory because it increases blood circulation and the flow of oxygen to the brain. This aids in brain function and brain cell regeneration, and this has an effect on memory. Exercise also helps control blood sugar levels.

This is important for memory function because people with impaired blood sugar levels have a smaller hippocampus, which is the area of the brain that controls memory.

Physical activity is also a powerful tool in the reduction of stress. Over production of stress hormones can have adverse effects on brain and memory function. Too much of the stress hormone cortisol can prevent the brain from accessing already existing memories and creating new memories.

IMPROVING MEMORY THROGH LOGICAL REASONING

Many people think they have a bad memory or simply cannot think straight. There are too many events which turn out that we forget something or neglect to prepare for the obvious, and this is allotted to a bad memory.

if it has nothing to do with memory at all but rather is the way thought is processed?

How often have you heard or said; "What were you thinking!" and the reply is the usual; "I don't know." How can you not know? That is unacceptable, and of course that reply is usually followed by more frustration for all concerned.

I would like to propose a possible solution and improvement to this common problem. The foundation of this article is that it is not really a bad memory that is the problem. Rather it is the thought process that does not take into account all the possible variables and potential aspects of the situation.

Basically, we do not consider everything that can happen and thus are ill prepared for the situation, then blame it on a bad memory because that is the habitual or commonly used excuse, right along with; "I guess I didn't think about it."

Exactly! We do not think, yet that same person who did not think has a brain that does function adequately or even extremely well at other times. And this is the point which gives me hope.

That my brain does work very well at times yet fails to function on even the simplest level at other times. Thus it cannot be my brain itself that is defective or limited, but something else that is causing the problem.

I will call the failing part the 'logical anticipation of probabilities.' Taking a recent example, a friend was coming over to my house to pick up a rather large item that I was storing for him. He showed up with a car already full of other stuff leaving no room to put in the package. His excuse was that he did not know how big the package he was collecting would be. That is a reasonable explanation but not a logical excuse.

The result was that he had to go back home again, empty his car, then come back again to pick it up. Had he applied logical reasoning, then he could have saved himself an extra trip. And it is from this last example that I have based this article.

Having owned several businesses, the lack of common sense was always a daily frustration. Why is it called 'common sense' when it is so very rare! The greatest frustration was, as I said before, simple errors were caused by people who otherwise acted very intelligently.

The explanation is that we did not think, yet the truth is that we did think, however we did not think about the probabilities of the situation. The intellect was thinking, but it was blinded from seeing the details.

There is a universal law we must take into account which is that everything we do is done for a reason. Whether you know the reason or not, or if the reason is a good or bad one, is irrelevant, there is always a reason.

The situation is that a person is given a task, they neglect to consider all the possibilities, and they fail to complete the task adequately. The excuse of not thinking is not valid since we are always thinking about something. Thus the solution is found in the question; "What were you thinking?"

To find the answer to that question, we must look at the source of our thoughts, which is our personality. Your brain does not 'think'. It is only an organ that processes thoughts and impulses.

It is your personality, who you are, that is doing the thinking. Those thoughts are sent to the brain and it then processes that information, which in turn results in your actions.

The next step is to determine your motivation for the things you think, or fail to think about. This brings us to the next universal law which is that the human design is to conserve energy, or in common terms of expression, to be lazy. The excuse given for laziness is 'trying to be efficient, to save time and money'. Cheap and lazy, results in extra time and cost!

If we accept that the universal laws of 'everything we do is done for a reason' and 'the human design is to conserve energy' effect all of us, we can then apply the other law of; 'My brain works sometimes, thus it can work all the time IF I know how to use it.'

And here is the key to using it well. The term I have always used to describe myself is that I am an 'optimistic pessimist'. I believe things will work out well, but at the same time I consider everything that can go wrong. This means I look at all the potential possibilities and am well prepared for every situation that could occur.

I learnt a great phrase from my flight instructor; "Better to have and not need than to need and not have."

This is such a simple process that it is a wonder why so many people do not follow it. And to this question I also have an answer: The devil is in the half truth.

There is a wide spread philosophy that we should always have positive thoughts. That is true. The problem is that taking this saying alone is only half the truth because it does not express that taking into account possible problems is NOT a negative thought.

It becomes a half truth because one eye sees the truth while we close the other eye to the reality of life on earth that, as Mr. Murphy said so well; "Anything that can go wrong, will go wrong."

This is not being negative, it is being objective. Have you ever tried closing one eye and looking around the room, or trying to work at your desk? So many things that were there are no longer visible. Just because you do not see it, does not mean it is not there.

Life does not change if we close one eye, it just gives us a big surprise when it bites your bum! Accept that there are always going to be issues or problems in every endeavor, and that will get your mind to start opening up because you will be willing to see all possibilities.

When your mind starts to open, you will be able to see the potential possibilities in every event. And the best part of this is that when you are accepting of reality and objectively considering the things that can go wrong, your mind will also be open to new ideas that can be done. You have now opened the door to pure creativity and invention.

STEPS TO IMPROVE YOUR CONCENTRATION POWERS

If you have the willpower you can easily learn the skill of mastering the power of concentration very ⬜uickly.

You've heard the saying," If there is a will, there is a way" the same holds true with concentration. Diane Sawyer is a very popular and well-known television news correspondent. When Diane was once asked about what has lead to her professional success, she had only one answer. That answer was being able to paying attention.

So the ⬜uestion still remains, "How do you learn to maintain your focus and enhance your concentration?"

The list below is helpful suggestions to improve your ability to concentrate in the most effective way possible. These tips apply whether you are at school, an important business meeting, at your office busy with work, or if you are just trying to finish a specific project.

1. Do five more

You are either one of two types of persons in this world. Either you know how to go through and eliminate frustration or you are the type that only wishes they are able to work through it.

So try to concentrate and focus in doing an additional five more things. This type of mantra is best used when you feel like giving up.

An example might be if you are reading or writing and you no longer want to continue to read or write, push yourself to do just five more pages. Complete five more math questions or if you are exercising add and extra five minutes on the treadmill.

Remember that athletes build their own physical physiques by pushing themselves to the point of exhaustion, that also helps to develop mental stamina.

2. Take one step at a time

There may be times when you feel like you are a scatterbrain because your mind is filled with many ideas. Controlling your brain is the key.

Do not worrying about lots of matters, prioritize tasks and do only those that are needed.

For instance, you cannot help but think of your mounting bill problems and this causes you to quit focusing on your presentation that needs to be done in five minutes. Tell yourself that after the presentation you can then focus on ways to pay off your bills. This gives your mind closure and allows you to focus completely on the presentation.

3. Get tunnel vision

You can actually cup your hands around your eyes and this could serve as a mechanism to tell your mind to stay on task.

Case in point: you are in a room and you need to study but there are many distractions preventing you from concentrating. Cupping your hands around your eyes will help your brain to remember to focus and keep it on task.

4. Keep a notepad handy

That way when a thought pops up and distracts your focus, you can write down the thought immediately.

By writing it down you effectively get the thought out of your mind. Now you will focus on the job that you need to accomplish at the moment.

5. Take a break

You are not a machine. You may need to take a break to be able to effectively focus on the job that you have to do.

You can mange the job more effectively by using breaks to break your tasks it to smaller parts. Try taking a walk outside or go out for lunch.

6. Record your start and end time

When doing work, try to record the time you started and the time that you loss focus.

This helps you know how much time you actually spent doing work and when you began losing your concentration. Being aware of this leads to understanding.

7. Mix up your activities

It is wise to change the activities you do so that you keep your mind alert and not bored.

A bored mind is not completely on its game and will wander.

All in all, these activities and suggestions should be practiced regularly to help you to be able to focus and concentrate on the things that really matter most to you.

IMPROVE YOUR MENTAL CONCENTRATION AND FOCUS

If you want to improve your mental concentration, have better mental focus, and enjoy stronger willpower so that you have more success in your life, then the fundamental skill you need to acquire is the ability to control your thoughts so that your mind works for your rather than against you.

Here, you'll learn three simple techniques that allow you to immediately begin controlling your thoughts. Plus, you can use the brain training exercises included in each suggestion to sharpen your thought control skills. So, the question is...

"WHAT DOES IT MEAN TO CONTROL THOUGHT?"

The power to control thought is the ability - at any given moment - to purposefully slow down and stop the busy, continuous movements of thoughts streaming through your mind.

To make that happen takes steady practice at paying close attention to thought itself, and making willful adjustments to ongoing thoughts to encourage positive effects, and prevent negative ones.

The results of doing so include ☐uiet relaxation, flawless efficiency, pleasant productivity, accelerated learning, self-confidence, deep creativity, masterful problem-solving, and a profound sense of well-being.

The very best way to master the habit (and get the benefits) of controlling your thoughts is a direct self-educating approach through mental fitness training; that is, regularly and consistently taking time out of your day exclusively to exercise your brain using strategic techniques that reshape and strengthen interconnecting pathways among brain cells.

This approach of neuro-sculpting (as opposed to 'body sculpting') affords you increased mental strength, endurance, and flexibility as you develop control and competence over previously untrained brain functions.

Brain training through dynamic mental fitness exercises is extremely practical in that it teaches you valuable lessons about aspects of your mind and thinking of which you are currently unaware. Among the first three things you discover during this approach are:

This direct, self-educating method of brain training exposes the rebellious nature of your untrained mind, revealing that despite our assumptions most of us don't have skillful control of our thoughts or our attention, the evidence of which becomes glaringly obvious once we attempt to command our mind to obey the orders of our will.

It reveals the shocking freƋuency of mental distractions rising up from your subconscious to assault your mind and perception all day long and into the night.

Finally, the process can immediately begin to give you control over all thoughts that are at the root of repetitive anxiety, stress, fear, and other power-draining negativities; thereby making room in your mind for you to create, foster, and manage the thoughts that bring you what you want in life, exclusively.

Intellectually, it may sound reasonable, but only through dedicated training will it really begin to make sense and fall into place in a way that proves you really can control your thoughts. Neuro-sculpting brain exercises reƋuire you to control thoughts in a very simple, basic way.

Through the small successes you achieve with dynamic mental fitness techniques, you get the necessary experiences that inspire you to confidently expand your efforts until your whole life begins to change for the better. Let's take a look at three techniques that can give you control over your thoughts:

METHOD ONE - SIGNAL INTERFERENCE

Method One is when you create a second thought WITHIN the first to break it up. You simply use something to interrupt the thought you don't want. When you practice this method, just sit and allow your mind to think whatever it will, then purposefully craft another thought while in the middle of the first.

For instance, if you are engaged in a thought about an office meeting, visualize a radio appearing out of thin air, blasting noisy music and disrupting the gathering. Focus in on the radio and it's music. Eventually, everything else will fade into the background, or fade away. You can think of plenty such scenarios.

METHOD TWO - SIGNAL DECAY

If you withhold your attention from becoming deeply involved with a thought, its signal is deprived of participatory energy it needs from you and degrades to fade away on its own in a matter of moments.

Signal decay is most popular in yoga and meditation wherein practitioners refuse to allow themselves to get caught up in the rough river of thoughts, and instead remain focused on an attentional target, such as the feel of their breathing, or a simple object like a candle flame.

One way you can practice this is to determine what your attention target will be, and when you find yourself assaulted by unwanted thought, focus in on your target, and hold your attention there by becoming extremely interested in the target so that you notice every detail about it.

Your mind will let go of whatever thought was bothering you in order to reallocate its resources to the new target, and without that energy, it dissolves.

METHOD THREE - SIGNAL DISPLACEMENT

You can eliminate an unwanted thought by willfully thinking another, competing thought. When you think the new thought, your mind will wrestle between the two, but if you are determined, the thought you create will inevitably crowd out the initial thought, thus displacing it.

You can try it by simple reaching back into your memory to recall a pleasant event and when you lock onto it, expand it in mind and immerse yourself into it in order to relive it.

Again, you may have to exert yourself, but the result is worth it, because you'll have real-time knowledge that you can stop one thought simply by resurrecting another. Do it repeatedly, and the rejected thought will lose its effect, and its existence.

For a life-changing self-education on controlling your thoughts, set aside a window of time each day for thirty days to practice the suggested techniues. At the end of the month-long period, you should be very familiar and capable of determining which thoughts you will allow and which thoughts you will no longer permit in your life.

WAYS TO BECOME A SUPER LEARNER

Enhancing memory and concentration is one thing that you may want to have to be able to do good in school or in your activities. Indeed, our mind's power can depend on many factors like nutrition, habits, lifestyle and attitude and yes, we can still find many ways on how to improve memory and concentration.

Although you can find many techniques on how to improve memory and concentration, it is also important to know the factors that affect your memory. It is important not to forget the basic needs of the body - the right nutrition and rest, because these greatly affect how your mind performs.

(1) Feed your body and mind with the right kinds of foods and enough rest. Make sure you have given your brain the fuel it needs to make it perform at its best. Fats from fish containing DHA and Omega 3 are said to be helpful in proper brain functioning.

Make your diet rich in vitamins and avoid caffeine and alcohol as concentration is best attained if you are relaxed. Do not skip breakfast. It will give your mind the energy to perform well throughout the day. Give it rest at times and make sure you get enough sleep to help you stay mentally focused.

(2) Learn how to meditate. Meditation involves deep breathing and some visualization that greatly helps in improving your concentration and memory. Meditation also allows you to relax, stay calm and reduce stress that you experience everyday. These things are important for you to be able to stay focused and sharpen your memory.

(3) Be attentive. Our memory works well if we have interest on a particular thing, subject or situation. If you want to learn how to improve memory and concentration, you have to also help yourself by being interested in activities that your do.

Learn to listen attentively and take a mental note of details. If you have listened to a speech, try remembering a line or sentences from that speech or from a conversation. The process of doing so will help you improve your concentration on the words of the speech.

(4) Identify your distractions and find ways to overcome them. Not being able to concentrate well may mean too many thoughts running in your mind or some distractions that prevent you to focus on one thing. If you are bothered with financial or emotional problems, work on overcoming them.

Also learn to control your thoughts. If multi-tasking is keeping you from concentrating, then do not do it. It does not really work with everyone.

(5) The power of repetition. Repeating the sentences you want to remember can also be a big help not just only in aiding your short-term memory but the long-term ones. Most often, if you tell a story to different people repeatedly, you tend to find it very easy to recall without even trying to exert too much effort and even if it has been while since you last told that story.

(6) Use some fun techniques on how to improve memory and concentration. You can find games that help you train your mind not only in improving focus and memory but also in improving your analytical skills.

For a better memory, you can also try the mnemonics techni ue to help you recall long items and lists. Adding a familiar tune or rhyme to the idea or concept you want to remember is another techni ue of helping your memory.

Essentially, there are basically two varied types of memory loss that you should be aware of when talking about how you remember. These are of course short term and long term memory loss.

And the former is really one of the more common ones within the circles of society and it refers to a very condition where individuals seem to forget certain things for short periods of time and some time later, they regain full memory of what they had misplaced in the annals of the mind in the first place.

One of the more common short term memory loss is experienced by women when they undergo pregnancy and this happens when there is a hormonal imbalance in the body to those proportions.

When the body goes into shock or a hormonal imbalance like pregnancy, the mind is affected directly and short term memory loss is one such ailment. Short term memory loss can also be described as loss of memory when concerning recent experiences.

For example, you will be able to remember events very clearly that happened years and years ago, but you may not be able to remember what you did yesterday or something that happened about a week ago.

This condition is also quite common to those who are suffering from short term memory loss and the problems that come with it can be quite disturbing. When not controlled, it can get progressively worse and worse, but of course normally, those who are suffering from this will experience the same sort of severity for a long time before it exacerbates.

Furthermore, it can be very, very frustrating and can be a problem in both your professional and your social life. Being at work and forgetting details is something that will either hamper your route to the top and can even get you fired in the first place. In your social life, this can have the same effect, just in different circumstances.

Still short term memory loss can be annoying and inflexible to covenant with. There are convinced things that you can do in order to conquer your memory defeat problems on the other hand. The primary obsession that somebody experiencing any sort of memory problems have to do is seek advice from their consultant.

This is significant since by undertaking a few straightforward tests your consultant will be proficient to conclude whether or not something more solemn is at play. There are plenty of other avenues you can pursue as well and this can include things like getting memory help tapes or even doing some simple mind memory exercises from the comfort of your own home.

Creating lists and reminders all over the house and do not be afraid of using technology like reminders on your PDA and hand phones to help you remember things.

With this, you can take away most of the problems that short term memory can be associated and sometimes, even overcome it completely. So be aware of the symptoms of short term memory loss, and take the necessary steps to overcome them before it is too late.

IMPROVE YOUR MEMORY WITH MNEMONICS

Mnemonics allows you to remember difficult and complex details which makes it useful when trying to learn how improve memory. Mnemonics are essentially rhymes as well as acronyms and they allow individuals to more easily memorize names and dates among other details.

How to improve the Memory using Mnemonics

Rhymes/Songs

Most people employ the use of the "30 days hath September" poem to memorize how many days there are in a month. Music has been employed by many individuals to help with memory improvement.

When hearing a mnemonic, the other person sitting next to you might not figure out what it is for but it will easily allow you to recall whatever that you want to. Strange and odd things tend to remain within your mind and mnemonics are just like that. That is why advertisers really use them. A product that has a song attached to it will be more easily noticed by a consumer.

Acronyms

In essence, your brain decodes a number of things that include touch, smell, sounds, structure and many other things which essentially take you towards memory increase. This information is then moulded together in the shape of the world as we see it.

Basically, this information is stored within our memories. Try to think of the world cloud and what it brings to your mind? Probably something white and fluffy. Mnemonics work in exactly the same manner. SCUBA is yet another mnemonic. Each letter signifies a distinctive word. Basically, it is an acronym that stipulates e□uipment used to breathe underwater.

Word Mnemonics/Acrostics

Individuals also utilize mnemonics to retain something as complex as the order of the universe. This is the order:Mercury, Venus, Earth, Mars, Jupiter, Saturn, Uranus, Neptune.

First of all, do not go any further and just try to retrieve the order to the planets by using the first letter in each of the names to make a handy sentence and figure out how to memorize quickly.

An example would be: My-Very-Eager-Mother-Just-Served-Us-Noodles. The key to creating mnemonic phrases is to be as creative as possible.

However, negative associations such as ones promulgating violence should be avoided because, above all, they tend to result in weak associations. Hence, go for positive mnemonics that make you think of great things and thus learn how improve memory.

Image Mnemonics

You can also use images as well as pictures to remind you of things. By coming up with a visualization of a particular situation, chances are you will easily remember it. Students use this particular method excessively because it allows them to memorize complex concepts.

In order to retain these images, they are drawn on lectures and slides by students who then are able to store them within their memory. All you have to ensure is the fact that you recall the meaning of the drawing.

Another useful suggestions involves creating images and memories that remind you of something that you have a lot of passion for. Funny pictures work best; people do not forget ridiculous incidents.

Also, you should try to mix acronyms with images to increase their effectiveness. In order to remember this, try thinking of a depressed bat. So why will you remember this image for a long time? Because it's pretty funny. You can also use images to remember people's names. As an example, think of the name John Horsely and then picture a horse's head?

Chaining/Linking

Essentially, chaining dictates the use and linking together of words to form a story. But do not confuse it with acrostics because chaining does not restrict you in regards to using extra words to give the story more sense. Chaining is perfect for people who have to retain and store in their minds large lists of items.

Basically mnemonics are used for helping people to remember complex info. Mnemonics can be used by a variety of people ranging from students to professionals.

SPEED LEARNING AND HOW OUR MEMORY WORKS

Speed learning is a very important skill that we need to master today. It is a person's fast track to success. If you want to take advantage of the millions of information that is made available to all of us today, you really need accelerated learning lessons.

Now, one of the basic things you need to know about speed learning is that your memory will play a huge role in your speed learning lessons. Don't worry though, a lot of speed learning teachers and courses will help you improve and sharpen your memory. But in order to make that easier for you, you have to understand first how our memories work.

Information flows from the outside world through our sight, hearing smelling, and tasting and touch sensors. Memory is simply ways we store and recall things we've sensed.

Recalling memories re-fires many of the same neural paths we originally used to sense the experience and, therefore, almost re-creates the event. Memories of concepts and ideas are related to sense experiences because we extract the essence from sensed experiences to form generalized concepts."

But to go into how our memory works, it usually involves three steps: encoding, storage and retrieval.

1) Encoding - consciously or subconsciously, new information is recognized by the brain but it is the important ones that are recorded into our memory. Normally, it is our brain that decides which ones are important. But with speed learning, you would be able to control which ones are important for you.

2) Storage - these are the methods used to create the recording of the new information that you have just inputted. This is also where your brain decides where the new information will be stored (short term, long term, etc.).

3) Retrieval - is where you would be applying the new information you have inputted and stored in your brain. There are many "triggers" involved in the retrieval of information. Most often than not, it would be emotional events that trigger this.

The brain is a very complicated piece of architecture. It's more complex than the most sophisticated computer chip and it is something that, in my opinion, cannot be fully understood even by the smartest scientists.

But with speed learning, you can apply some techniques that would help you make the most out of what's already known and understood about the brain. There are a lot of speed learning techniques and information that would help you improve yourself and the way your brain handles new information.

accelerated learning will also help you harness your memory and your intelligence. With speed learning, you will really get the chance to reach your full potential.

To compete in today's quick-moving, information-intense society, a good memory is an important quality to possess. The ability to remember important pieces of information like names, faces, facts, dates, events, and other components of daily life is vital to your success.

If you have a good memory, you won't need to worry about forgetting or losing important items, and you can overcome mental blocks that prevent you from achieving your maximum potential on the job, at home, and in your love life.

Your memory is controlled by a complex network of interconnected neurons within the brain that can hold millions of pieces of independent data. It is this ability of your mind to store detailed, organized memories of past experiences that makes you capable of learning and creativity.

These experiences stored in the form of memories help you learn from mistakes, protect you from danger, and achieve the goals that you set. By harnessing the power of your memory, you are better able to learn life lessons that help you avoid mistakes in the future based on your own past and the failures of others.

While poor memory can sometimes be the result of a mental handicap or disability, it most often has to do with a lack of attention or inability to concentrate, poor listening skills, and other types of bad habits.

Fortunately, you can re-train yourself with proper habits to develop and fine-tune your memory. The basic tool for developing better memory is the "clustering" technique.

Examples of clustering include:

1. Grouping by numbers, letters, physical characteristics, or categories

2. Grouping words and concepts that are related, or opposites

3. Grouping with mental pictures or subjective organization

Data clustering improves memory by breaking information into more easily manageable pieces. For example, consider a 10-digit phone number with area code. By memorizing the numbers in groups of three or four, you'll be able to more easily access this data from your memory bank.

Word or concept clustering involves grouping words together in our minds to help us have better recollection. This harnesses the power of association, in which one thought or suggestion leads you to recall another. One example is word pair clusters. These can be synonyms, antonyms, or associated words. For example "fair" and "s uare", "man" and "woman".

Clustering through subjective organization uses categories, processes, devices, and associations to remember data.

For example, vocabulary words are often remembered in groups, based on the context in which they were discussed. Remembering one word triggers the memory of an unrelated word with which it was somehow grouped or associated.

Let's take cooking as another example. While there are a number of ingredients in a recipe, each one of these individual ingredients has no context by itself. It's only through the process of combining each of these ingredients that the whole context takes shape.

In sum, use the following strategies to hone your memory:

1. Reflect on the process of problem solving or contextualizing instead of trying to memorize facts out of context.

2. Understand what techniques work best for you individually. Do you work best with category clusters? Or are you more visually driven?

3. Analyze situational details and experiences to remember important data, and eliminate unnecessary data

COMBINING SHORT AND LONG TERM MEMORY
FOR INSTANT RECALL

Upon experiencing a particular sensation, be it a pleasurable sound, sight or smell, the stimuli is flashed in the sensory regions of the brain. If the brain focused on the stimuli consciously, mainly due to the activity in the thalamus, the sensations registered are then transferred to short term memory storage in the cerebral cortex.

The information that is stored in short term memory is simply a collection of electrochemical connections between neurons. In order to make a permanent imprint into long term memory, it is necessary for the connections to remain during the transfer between the short term memory regions of the brain to the long term memory regions of the brain.

This transfer process is largely driven by the hippocampus and it was shown that sleep plays a major role in this consolidation.

Furthermore, recent studies employing neuroimaging suggest that certain brain activation patterns during sleep appear to be identical to those observed during the learning session that preceded it-propounding that the brain automatically performs a certain type of repetition during sleep in order to consolidate the memory.

To consciously keep the electrochemical connections active whilst the transfer between short to long term memory is taking place, re□uires a strategy- it commonly involves:

Repetition- which re-enforces the electrochemical connections.

Analysis- which forces one to create a logical link to information that is already in long term storage.

Emotional reaction- the pathways are encoded much more strongly as the emotional response is included in the registered sensation.

Mnemonic- an artificial link that tricks the brain into remembering, fre□uently combining the 3 factors above to provide a more powerful encoding approach.

These methods stimulate the frontal lobes and cause a protein synthesis in the neural connections which then fixes the information in long term storage.

The education system tends to focus on using Repetition and Analysis though with some experimentation it becomes evident that these methods are slow and dull- thus making the whole learning experience sub-optimal and less enjoyable.

Mnemonics and memory systems have been used to assist learning as far back as the days of Simonides of Ceos and possibly even before that in ancient Egypt.

The techniques have evolved substantially over time and applications were developed to suite new data types; however, the underlying principles remain the same.

The key to such systems is to use creativity and imagination in a very specific manner- combining information that is unknown with something that is already known.

The technique demonstrated below is the most basic application of such systems yet it is extremely powerful and effective. As an example, say one wishes to apply the memory principles to remember foreign language vocabulary. The steps of the technique are as follows:

Convert the foreign language word to something you can visualise- this involves finding a similar sounding word (or words) that you already know.

Convert the word into an item you can visualise- if it is an object then this is easy, if it not, one can find a similar sounding word as above or use an object that reminds you of the word.

Then in your mind's eye, combine the two images using exaggeration or nonsensical action- the key here is to make the resulting image something absurd that you would not expect to encounter in reality.

Example:

The Chinese word for Apple is píng guo;

The Chinese word can be substituted with "Ping Goal"- "Ping" can be visualised as a Ping-Pong ball whilst "Goal" can be visualised as a soccer goal.

The translation word, apple, is simple to visualise- just think of the last time you have eaten this fruit.

To combine the images, begin by visualising a gigantic green apple (try to sense how crunchy it feels); then proceed by visualising that apple on a soccer field kicking a Ping Pong ball and scoring a Goal. Exaggerate the image making sure that the apple and the ping pong ball are out of proportion compared to the way that they exist in reality.

Hold that image in your mind, ensuring colour and feelings are incorporated into the scene; it should be an image that arouses emotion- in the example above it should make you lightly amused or even laugh.

In order to recall the information, all that is re uired is that you let the image pop to your mind as you hear either the foreign word or its translation.

For instance, as you are crossing China-Town you hear a street vendor calling out "ping guo", what image comes to your mind? If you followed the steps above you should see an apple kicking the ping pong ball- thus reminding you that the meaning of píng guo is apple.

This is a very fast, simple, enjoyable and effective way of instantly storing new information. With some modifications, these simple concepts can be applied to memorizing any type of information.

SIMPLE MEMORY TECHNIQUES FOR REMEMBERING NAMES

The world memory champion can memorize 170 names and faces in 15 minutes. Yet many people cannot recall a single name thirty seconds after hearing it.

If we stay conservative for a moment and assume that remembering 170 names is the best people will ever be able to do, it should still be a piece of cake to remember one name of a person who just introduced herself to you three minutes ago. Right?

Wrong. All too often the name slips out of the mind, even after you ask for it the second time around.

Then a week later you see her walking down the street and you want to call out and say hi. Except there is no name in your mind. I used to devise clever strategies for finding out the name second and third time around without asking for it directly:

- "Let me see the photo on your driver's license."

- "So, how do your close friends call you?"

- "You have an unusual name, how do you pronounce it?" (and hope she doesn't say "Kate")

- "What do they call you in this country?" (works well with foreigners)

- Hang around and wait until someone else pronounces her name. This strategy fails if the name is foreign and complicated - you hear it but cannot repeat it.

Wouldn't it be nice if you could easily and effortlessly memorize anyone's name in just a few seconds?

Better yet capture the names of a whole group of people as you are introduced to them and remember them once and for all. If the world champion can do it with 170 names, you can certainly do it with five or ten or even twenty.

Let us first examine what is involved in storing and recalling information in your mind, and then I will come back to the specific name remembering strategy. There are three phases to storing information:

-Attention. You have got to pay attention to the information by listening, watching, sensing. Have you ever had an experience of reading a book while preoccupied with other thoughts, like the parking ticket you got in the morning? How much of what you have read did you remember afterwards?

Rampant self talk is the biggest obstacle to having a great memory. You need anywhere from 3 to 15 seconds of active (!) attention to form a strong memory in your mind. (If you have an outstanding power of concentration, you only need 2 seconds or 1 second or even less.

-Strategy. Use an effective memory strategy. There are many great ones that work really well, yet most people keep using truly awful strategies they picked up accidentally along the way when growing up.

For example, if you want to remember a telephone number, mental tape loops when you keep saying the number to yourself over and over again are a particularly poor memory strategy. (Especially so if you remembered the number in one language, and someone

There is not a single memory strategy appropriate for everything. You need to learn a few to handle all sorts of situations.

Some of them have been invented many millennia ago. For example, a very effective memory strategy for giving long speeches without the help of written notes was created by Greek orators. I will describe a great name remembering strategy in a second.

-Neurology. Neurologically record the memory in your brain. Occasionally, these neurological processes can be affected by certain physiological conditions (powerful drugs, physical brain damage, or some rare disorders), but this is usually the rarest cause when people complain of poor memory.

Recalling information has one phase:

- See, hear or sense the trigger and recall the information. It does you no good to remember just the names - you have a name, but no face. You must associate the two together, so that the face triggers the recall of the name.

We automatically take care of this in the name remembering strategy below. But for other times, make sure you create a recall trigger that naturally occurs in your environment or that you have easy access to (e.g. do not connect all of your math learnings to the textbook or your notes - you will not have access to them during the test).

BULLETPROOF NAME REMEMBERING STRATEGY

I used to think that remembering names was hard. My strategy was to listen to the name and ... that's it. Not much of a strategy, but I did have a handful of how-to-get-the-name-a-second-time-around strategies. Then I learned how to do it properly and easily.

First, pay attention to the person saying their name. Do not look around, do not think about your dinner plans. Do look at them directly for at least 3 seconds. I typically handshake for 3 seconds while making eye contact.

Listen to the name and imagine it written in large bright letters around their head. Keep this image in your mind for 3 to 15 seconds, depending on your power of concentration. While seeing the image, say the name to yourself in their voice three times. With your free hand write the name on your hip or in the air (keep your hand movements small and unobservable). That's it.

HOW DOES IT WORK

Notice that the bulletproof name remembering strategy uses all three of your sensory channels - visual, auditory and kinesthetic. The result is a synergy. If you were to use only one of the three channels, visual is by far the most important one for most people.

Here is a tip - when I learned this strategy, initially it did not work for me. I was told to write the names on the forehead. I did and I did not remember them. Then I discovered through experimentation that my letters were too small, I could not make them out afterwards. The key is to make the imaginary writing big and bright.

REMEMBERING MANY NAMES AT A TIME

We will use the chunk & review method. Have you heard of psychologist George A. Miller's 7+-2 memory chunks? He discovered in 1956 that people on average can keep in their short-term memory seven plus or minus two chunks of information.

If more information is given to them, something else must be forgotten before the new information is recorded. So if you want to remember more then 7+-2 names, you need to transfer the first set from the short-term to the long-term memory.

Suppose you are being introduced to a group of twenty people. We are going to memorize their names in chunks of five. Start by memorizing the first five names using the bulletproof name remembering strategy.

Then pause and chunk this information by reviewing all five names in ⬚uick succession (look at each one of the first five people and mentally say their name). Then continue by memorizing the next five names, pause, chunk & review. Simple.

BETTER VISION FOR IMPROVED MEMORY

Exploring the world, enjoying our daily activities, and experiences. Can you imagine how bleak the world would be without our eyes? From this point of view, it makes sense to take our eye care more seriously. A great way to do this is to start devoting as much attention to the care of our eyes as we would regular physical exercise.

Eye exercises provide a series of benefits. Besides relieving stress and tension in the visual system, they also promote sharper, clearer, natural eyesight. However, a surprising benefit of eye exercises that you would not expect is that some techniques do provide the additional benefit of improving memory.

Here is one such eye technique: The main objective of this particular exercise is to hold the memory of a visual object in your mind for as long as you possibly can. Hold up a book and select a letter on a page of that book. Choose a large letter. Then cover one eye lightly either with your hand or an eye patch. Glance quickly at the letter with the open eye.

Then, close both eyes as you visualize the image of the letter you selected. Let it remain in your mind for as long as possible. As you are performing this technique, count the number of seconds that the letter remains in your mind until eventually,it starts to fade away in your imagination.

Make a note of the length of time in terms of the number of seconds you were able to retain that image in your mind. Record it by writing it down in a note book. Each consecutive time, try to retain the image of the letter for longer periods of time.

Here is another technique that not only relieves eye strain but also improves memory, enhancing mental function. You can perform this technique by relaxing your eyes. A great way to relax the eyes is to focus on pleasant positive thoughts.

Think about some of the most memorable occasions in your life. It could be a wedding, a graduation, your favorite vacation. Dwell on these positive events. Forget about all your worries, troubles and cares.

Vision and memory are connected. For instance, in the case of the memory exercise described earlier, you needed your vision in order to see the image you were concentrating on. The memory exercise also helps you remember details. Details you will be able to recall later.

Always focus on positive things that are happening in your life. This is important as it helps you to relax the eyes and eliminate eye strain. Vision, stress relieving eye techniues and memory are all inter-related in some way.

Here is another natural eye exercise that will eliminate eye strain and also improve your memory. You can try this technique before going to bed. Try to recall all of the positive things that happened to you throughout the day.

While reviewing these positive events in your mind, focus on them with as much detail as possible. For example, if someone complimented you on your work performance or your appearance dwell on these events.

A positive mental focus euals positive mental health. It's benefits go beyond vision improvement, contributing to better memory. You may be wondering what positive thinking has to do with memory. More than you can imagine.

A positive mental attitude puts you in a relaxed state and this state improves our learning ability. For example, saying to yourself, I am excited about having good sharp memory, ties in with the confidence that you have about your memory.

A negative mental focus on the other hand contributes to stress which hinders memory. This locks out our mind's ability to record information.

Relaxation techniques, eye exercises, a positive mental focus, and memory all play an integral role in maintaining our eye health. Include all these elements into your eye exercise routine and you'll achieve better eye health and memory.

CONCLUSION

So how do you improve memory capability? Just so you know, your lifestyle and behavior have a big impact on how properly you are able to produce new memories. Your memories not only describe things from your past, known as your long-term memory, but also pertains to your short-term memory.

A person's short-term memory is where you actually hold information like names, addresses, some phone numbers, grocery checklist, and so on. Anybody can benefit from improving their memory.

If you want to improve your memory, you need to make sure to stay positive. When you constantly tell yourself that you will not be able to remember something, then you probably won't. Spending your time thinking negatively won't help at all.

Exercise your memory instead by doing mental activities such as playing crossword puzzles, chess, or learning a new language or playing a musical instrument.

It is also important that you make a conscious effort to get it locked in your head that you are not afraid of forgetting. This adjustment of your attitude is one of the first and easiest ways on how you can improve your memory.

Another factor is that a person's memory and alcohol have a fascinating connection. Based on research, there's information that light to modest alcohol consumption can help enhance one's memory and cognition. Too much drinking, however, hinders your memory's capability.

Some research shows that reasonable drinkers have had far better performance on particular assessments on memory than non-drinkers or intense drinkers.

Additionally, one of the flavonoids in red wine, which is thought to have special benefits regarding blood vessels, and subsequently, memory, can also be found in red grape juices.

It also contains lots of antioxidants which are very helpful to our body, especially our brain cells, as it protects against cell damage, making our brain and memory function properly.

One other way you improve memory is by making sure to keep your stress level down. As anxiousness or anger make its way into our lives, some portions of our brain which are responsible for storing and developing memories are slowly but surely eaten away.

Depression can really affect memory. Depressive disorders have been misidentified as a memory issue since one of the major symptoms of this condition is the inability to concentrate.

Whenever an individual doesn't possess the ability to concentrate on things like their schoolwork or their job, it can be stressful. Managing that stress properly can really help resolve the cause of the stress itself.

c

These are just some of the ways on you can improve memory by changing or modifying your behavior. What you do really affects what you can be.